TRUST GOD!

From a Mother's Grief to
Affirming Faith: How God
Gives Us Twice As Much

KEEBA SMITH

20Twenty
Literary Group

ISBN
978-1-961250-32-1 (Paperback)
978-1-961250-33-8 (eBook)
978-1-961250-31-4 (Hardcover)

To my parents and my wonderful husband, for loving me unconditionally.

To my children, for being the prides and joys of my life.

To Mrs. Wanda Benson, for giving me something special: your time.

Table of Contents

In Loving Memory of
Nancy Jean Kaye Richardson

July 22, 2004- October 31, 2006

Rest in peace my
precious daughter

Introduction

In November 2006, I was sitting in the waiting area of my therapist's office. While waiting, a woman entered and sat down. She appeared to be overly- anxious and exhausted. I am not much of a conversationalist, but since she seemed troubled, I was compelled to say something to her. After getting her attention I asked, *Are you alright?* She replied, *I am exhausted from work and I have a million things to do. The only reason I am here is because of court ordered anger management.* I replied, *Okay.* She then asked me my age. I didn't get offended because usually when I'm asked this question, it is because I look younger than I am. I take it as a compliment. I replied, *I will be 27 next week.* She scoffed and said, *Honey, you are still a child. You haven't even begun to have any pain and suffering.* After that encounter, her statement resonated in my spirit for a while. I asked myself: *When did trials, tribulations, pain and suffering have an age limit?* Should we as a society tell a child who loses a parent to get over it because they are not old enough to feel pain or heartache? Should we say to a child who was molested, *Don't worry about it. You're too young to be traumatized by that experience.* Of course we would not say this. It would be insensitive and would show lack of compassion to say such a thing- especially to a child. The fact is that trials and tribulations, as well as pain and suffering have no age limit or expiration date. This book seeks to explain how heartache, struggles, pain and discouragement can be used for good. In this life, we all will go through the various emotions that make us human-joy, pain, laughter, sorrow, happiness, anger, but the key is how we respond to such things. If we allow those emotions to do what they were intended to do-make us stronger, wiser, build character and teach us humbly, then we become better; but if we do not allow the lessons to be learned by becoming better, we get stuck in those places and never grow.

MY TESTIMONY

*The Lord Gives and the Lord takes away. Blessed
be the name of the Lord. (Job 1:21)*

The premature death of my daughter had me in grief counseling. On October 31, 2006, my two year-old daughter, Nancy Jean Kaye Richardson, was hit by a car and later died at the hospital. She was my only child at the time and since her father and I were not together anymore, I was raising her alone. She was my world. I remember that dreadful day as though it were yesterday. I had picked Nancy Jean up from daycare around 3:30 pm., then we went to my parent's house. I combed her hair and had laid her Halloween costume out in preparation for trick or treating later on. She was going to be Barney, which was her favorite character. My mother was a teacher at the elementary school directly across the street and would normally get off work at 4:30p.m. daily. While in the side yard playing with my 11 year-old niece, Nancy Jean looked up and saw my mother walking across the street coming home. In her excitement to see her grandmother, she ran towards her, out into the street as a car was coming and was struck by a car. She was rushed to a local hospital where they ran several tests and a CT scans to make sure there was no bleeding in her head. We were told by the doctor that she was okay and that everything was fine, but to be safe, the doctor had her transported by helicopter to The University Medical Center in Jackson, Mississippi for observation. She seemed to be okay. She was alert and responsive. With a helicopter transport, they normally would not allow anyone to ride with a patient as they are being transported, but that night, they allowed me to ride with her. While on the way there, she flat lined. The paramedics desperately tried all that they could do to revive her to no avail. Once we landed, she was rushed into the pediatric emergency room where they were able to revive her. A full body scan revealed that her liver and spleen had been ruptured. She was sent to emergency surgery but died on the operating table from a hemorrhaged liver. It was a Tuesday. She was buried that Saturday.

The Process

After my daughter's death, I went through a series of emotions, which I later learned was called the five stages of grief: denial, anger, bargaining, depression, and acceptance. During the first stage, Denial and Isolation: I kept wishing that what had happened was a bad dream that I was going to wake up from at any moment. During this time, I just wanted to be alone and did not want to be around anyone. I was in a very dark pace and life seemed to be passing me by. I could not think clearly and was trying to wrap my head around the reality of what had happened. There were those who tried to reach out to me out of love, care and concern, but I simply wanted to be left alone. The pain was unbearable and I could not understand what had happened, why it had happened or if it had really happened.

When the reality of what had happened actually hit me and I had to face the fact that it was not a dream, then anger emerged.

I wasn't sure who to be angry with at first, so I targeted the anger towards myself for allowing her to play outside. I blamed myself for her death and hated myself for what had happened. I felt like a good mother would never have allowed their child to play outside, even though she had played outside a thousand times. I then directed the anger towards my mother for not driving to work instead of walking that day. Of course, the anger transferred to the driver for being on that side of town; and then my anger was directed at God for giving Nancy Jean to me only to take her back so soon. I felt as though I had been robbed by God. I felt that God was supposed to be loving and kind, not allow heartache like this to happen to His children. When I transitioned to the Bargaining Stage, I kept telling God that I would gladly trade my life for hers and to just make this situation a bad dream. I would have given up anything for her to be with me on earth again. I was still praying that what I was having a bad dream, but I would be sorely disappointed when I continued to realize that it was my reality. When depression sunk in, it had me experiencing periods of blackouts and heavy drinking. I did not want to get out of bed. I just wanted to lay there and wallow in my misery and self-pity. There were many days of heavy crying, heavy drinking, severe depression, and even suicidal thoughts at times but I eventually I moved on to stage five, the Acceptance stage. I reached a point where I was finally able to accept that my baby was gone and never coming back. I had to accept that this was God's Will and that He knows what's best for me. I began embracing the fact that since she was not old enough to have committed any sins, she had to be in the Father's presence and that she was experiencing full joy and happiness. This thought gave me comfort and strength to move on. It was still bad and the pain was still there, but with each passing day, the pain became more bearable.

Was my suffering any less painful because I was 26? A young mother who loses a child goes through the same five stages of grief as an older mother who loses a child. A child who loses their parents is called an orphan. A person who loses their spouse is called a widow or widower. But what do you call a parent who loses a child? There is no name for that because it is an unnatural occurrence. A parent should not have to bury their child. That is not the natural order of things. Someone once asked me how I made it through that difficult time in my life? I had only one answer, "By the Grace of God." He never gives you more than you can bear.

"No temptation has overtaken you except what is common to mankind. And God is faithful; he will not let you be tempted beyond what you can bear. But when you are tempted, he will also provide a way out so that you can endure it." 1 Corinthians 10:13

(New International Version)

Lessons Learned

- God gives and God takes away, blessed be the name of the Lord
- The Lord is my strength and my shield, a very present help in trouble
- Blessed are they that mourn, for they shall be comforted.

TRIALS & TRIBULATIONS

I have told you these things, so that in me you may have
peace. In this world you will have trouble. But take
heart! I have overcome the world (John 16:33).

Everyone must experience trouble at some point in their lives. Many refer to these troubles as "trials and tribulations", but the question that some might ask is, "What are trials and tribulations?" The dictionary defines them as great afflictions, distress or suffering. A second definition refers to them as *an experience that test one's endurance, patience, or faith.* Anytime we have problems or difficulties that we encounter, then we are experiencing the effects of trials and/or tribulations. No one is exempt from having trials and tribulations.

In the chapter's opening scripture, Jesus is saying to us that as long as we are in this world, we will have tribulations, but we can find peace in Him if we seek it. We may find joy in the fact that He overcame the world, which means that whatever we go through while in this world, Jesus has already overcome it for us. It may be easy for one person to say to another not to focus on the world or the problems we face in the world if that person has no problems of their own at the moment; but as believers in Christ, we know that our problems are only temporary. However, while we are in the center of them, it is not so easy to NOT focus on the effects of those problems. It is easy to quote a word to make others feel better, but much more difficult to walk in what we quote at times when we ourselves are going through. Yet, I will say that although we may experience some trials and tribulations that may knock us down to our knees, we may always find hope and peace in Jesus. If we would just take our focus off of the problems for a moment and focus on the Lord, He will give us the peace and strength we need to get through the problem, trial, tribulation, hurt, grief we face. As a way maker, He will make a way. We find it easy to thank God for our successes and blessings, but we must also thank Him for our failures because our failures may also show us who we truly are or even help to make us humble. As I write this line, a quote comes to mind that was spoken by Arthur Ashe: *"Happiness keeps you sweet. Trials keep you strong. Sorrow keeps you human. Failure keeps you humble. Success keeps you glowing, but only God keeps you going."* When we put our trust in man and the world that is when most of our trials and tribulations come because man will always fail us. Troubles usually come when we take our focus off of the Master. You may see losing your job, your house, your marriage, or even death of a loved one as a failure or hardship or an unbearable loss, but sometimes God has to do things to get our attention. We must understand that as believers of Christ and children of God, all things do work together for our good; not some things, but ALL things. In our limited, finite minds, we may not be able to comprehend how losing a loved one, losing a job or experiencing a devastating tragedy could work together for good, but an infinite and unlimited God has ordained from the foundation of the world that it would be so. He has the power to redeem the time and give you back everything you lost and more, if you would only trust Him. Whatever you are going through may not feel good but it is working together for your good.

"And we know that in all things god works for the good of those who love him, who have been called according to his purpose." Romans 8:28 (New International Version)

Since we may not be able to change the situations or circumstances that enter our lives, we change our view of those trials and tribulations below:

Scenario:

1. An employee has worked eight hours of hard labor and before he clocks out, he is called to the supervisor's office to be told that the company is experiencing an economic downturn and they have to lay him off. The employee walks to his car and sits there shocked and discouraged. He is worried about what he is going to do for money, how is he going to pay the bills and provide for his family? He has to pay the mortgage, car notes, insurances, child care, utility bills, credit cards, and etc. He worries and begins to wonder if unemployment benefits will be enough to cover his expenses. He is frustrated because he doesn't know what he is going to do. The frustration begins to escalate and his emotions begin to take over as his thoughts take him to places that are dark and depressing.

2. An employee has worked eight hours of hard labor and before he clocks out, he is called to the supervisor's office to be told that the company is experiencing an economic downturn and they have to lay him off. The employee walks to his car and sits there shocked and discouraged, but then he begins to pray. "Father I thank you God for eight years of a job that allowed me to care for my family and pay my bills. Thank you Father that while on that job, I have learned new skills that I can take with me wherever

I go. I now put my trust in you Lord; for I cannot see in the natural where I am going to get money to continue paying my bills and caring for my family, but I know that you are going to make a way. I trust you and I trust your word when you said that you would never leave me nor forsake me. So Father, in spite of what just happened, I will still thank you because in your Word it says in everything, give thanks. I am asking for guidance, insight, and foresight into the next phase of my life. I trust that there is another job waiting for me that is better than the one I am leaving and I thank you for it in advance.

These are the two identical scenarios with two completely different responses. The difference was that they had two different outlooks over their situation because one had the Lord in his heart and He knew to cast his cares upon Him. The first man worried about money and bills. His focus was not on Jesus. The second man prayed. He trusted that the Lord would make a way. If you are going pray, then there is no need to worry. If you are going to worry, then there is no need to pray. If you are going to pray and worry at the same time, then you are not trusting God to do what He said he would do and your prayer are in vain. Praying and worrying are like oil and water, they do not work together. Many Christians go through periods of doubt and unbelief. We all do at times, but we must get to a place where our faith supersedes our doubt and unbelief and we begin walking as though our prayers have already been answered. God can move mountains, but faith and prayer can move God. Mark 9:24 *"I do believe; help me overcome my unbelief."* (New International Version)

It is written in the Word for everything that has breath to praise the Lord. We commanded to praise our Maker and Creator, but all too often, we praise the creation instead of the Creator. We often get it backwards, but when we make a habit to pray and praise God whether we are encouraged or discouraged, we get to a place where we are no longer moved by worldly issues. We begin to see that if we lose something or someone, it is because God takes things from us so that He can bless us with something better. If you trust and believe in God, He will bless you with twice as much as you had before. In order to gain something, we must give up something, but when we make the sacrifice to give up something, God replaces it with something better.

Lessons Learned

- Troubles usually come when we take our focus off of the Master.
- It is the failures that protect us from going in the wrong direction at times.
- When we put our trust in man and the world, that is when most of our trials and tribulations come
- Success keeps you glowing, but only God keeps you going.

THE STORY
OF JOB

*Naked came I out of my mother's womb, and naked shall
I return thither. The Lord gave, and the Lord hath taken
away; blessed be the name of the Lord! (Job 1:21)*

The book of Job tells the story of a man who loses everything -
his wealth, his family, and even his health. He wrestles with the
question, "Why?" According to the Bible, Job was a perfect and
upright man that feared God and shunned evil. The story begins
with a heavenly debate between God and Satan in Job 1:7-12

> *7:The Lord said to Satan, "Where have you come
> from?" Satan answered the Lord, "From roaming
> throughout the earth, going back and forth on it."*

> *8: Then the Lord said to Satan, "Have you considered
> my servant Job? There is no one on earth like him;
> he is blameless and upright, a man who fears God
> and shuns evil."*

9: "Does Job fear God for nothing?" Satan replied.

10: "Have you not put a hedge around him and his household and everything he has? You have blessed the work of his hands, so that his flocks and herds are spread throughout the land.

11: But now stretch out your hand and strike everything he has, and he will surely curse you to your face."

12: Then the Lord said to Satan, "Very well, then, everything he has in your power, but on the man himself do not lay a finger."

We learn a lot about both Satan and God in this debate. The first thing we learn is that Satan is here on earth roaming about and he can take on many shapes and forms. Satan knows mostly everything about us and he knows our weaknesses. He takes whatever form or shape is necessary to target that weakness. In Matthew 4:1-11, we read that while Jesus was on a forty days and forty nights fast, He was tempted. This was during a most vulnerable time. He was hungry and physically weak. The devil tempted Jesus in the area of his weakness, which was his flesh at the time by telling him to turn stones into bread. He knew that Jesus was hungry, so the devil tempted him in the area that he would be most likely to give in, but Jesus used the Word of God to fight his enemy. His response was, *"Man shall not live by bread alone, but by every word of God."* The enemy did leave, but came back with a second temptation, which was to tempt Jesus to throw himself down from the pinnacle of the temple. The devil even used the Word of God to support his request: "for it is written, He shall give his angels charge concerning thee: and in their hands they shall bear thee up, lest at any time thou dash thy foot against a stone." This shows us that even the devil knows the Word of God but he distorts it, then tries to use it to his advantage. Jesus used the word rightly in response to Satan's request: *"For it is written, though shall not tempt the Lord thy God."* The third and final temptation was when the devil tried to get Jesus to bow down and worship him. *"Again, the devil taketh him up into an exceeding high mountain, and shewth him all the kingdoms of the world, and the glory of them; And saidth unto him, All these things will I give thee, if thou wilt fall down and worship me. Then saidth Jesus unto him, Get thee hence, Satan: for it is written, Thou shalt worship the Lord thy God, and him only shalt thou serve,"* (Matthew 4:8-10). Jesus is the Son of God. After failing to tempt Jesus three times, the devil left for a season and the angels came and attended to Jesus. If Satan will tempt Jesus, the Maker and Creator of the entire world, and Job, a man who was right in the eyes of God, then he will certainly tempt us. Satan wants us to curse God as he tried to tempt Job to do. However, God is our protector. He gives us the strength that we need in His Word to fight the devil and win. We must fear God and rebuke evil. Satan wants us to turn away from God and turn towards him. We saw in the passage above that he wants our worship. He will do everything in his power to turn us away from God. However, there is one thing about Satan's power that we must realize. He can not do anything to us that God doesn't allow. We can look at what we are experiencing as Satan's doing or God's Will. If God is allowing Satan to do something in our lives then it is all according to his will and his purpose. We win in the end.

In the course of one day, Job receives four messages. First, the message that he loses his oxen and donkeys comes. Second, the message that he loses his sheep and servants comes. Third, the message that he loses his sons and daughters comes. When he gets the message that his cattle was gone, he realizes that he has lost his job and his livelihood but when He loses all seven of his sons and three daughters, that was a message that was utterly devastating and deeply heartbreaking. His world was ripped apart in one day. If we have never experienced anything remotely close to what happened to Job, we can only imagine the magnitude of his devastation and anguish from such an experience. We have all had those days when Murphy's Law (Anything that can go wrong will go wrong) seems to take over, but have you ever experienced Murphy's Law to that magnitude? Job fell down in worship.

In life, everything is about responses. Job's response to all of his loses spoke volumes about his character: *"Naked I came from my mother's womb, and naked I will depart. The Lord gave and the Lord has taken away; may the name of the Lord be praised."(Job 1:21).* Job knew that everything he had owned was given to him by God. People oftentimes believe that the things they have were acquired on their own merit and strength but the reality of it is that, they have nice things because God gave them a job to be able to afford nice things. God can also take that job away. We, as Christians should embrace the mindset that material things don't have any eternal life value. There is nothing wrong with having nice things but it is important what type of value is placed on them. I remember one day when I was younger, my sister and I were sitting in the backseat of my parents' car. My father was driving and mother was in the passenger seat. My sister and I had Cherry flavored Kool-Aid packages. We ended up wasting them all over the backseat. My father was angry with us. He did not spank us very often but we got a major spanking that day because my father prized his car. My sister and I are both adults now and we view material things differently. My sister drives an expensive luxury car and one my niece wasted some soda in it. My sister pulled over to the side of the road, spanked her and made her clean it up. That same niece was in the car with me and accidently squirted ketchup all over my back seat. When I pulled over to clean it up, she started crying and apologizing. I told her that it was okay and that it was only ketchup. She later asked me why I did not spank her. I told her that it was just a car and that I cannot take it to heaven when I leave here, so I don't prize material things. And besides, we all make mistakes. She smiled. That moment to me was priceless. The only thing that has true eternal value is our soul. Job realized this, hence his statement about God giving and God taking away.

"What good will it be for someone to gain the whole world, yet forfeit their soul? Or what can anyone give in exchange for their soul?" Matthew 16:26 (New International Version)

If we were more like Job, we would realize that everything we have comes from God. Job lost everything imaginable and yet he still worshipped God. So even during your bad times and heartaches, praise God! In the midst of your storm, praise God! While you are waiting for a door to open, praise Him in the hallway. We have to find joy in the little things and trust in the Lord.

If we review to the story of Job in chapter 2:2-6, God and Satan are having another heavenly debate about Job.

> *2: And the Lord said to Satan, "Where have you come from?" Satan answered the Lord, "From roaming throughout the earth, going back and forth on it."*

> *3: Then the Lord said to Satan, "Have you considered my servant Job? There is no one on earth like him; he is blameless and upright, a man who fears God and shuns evil. And he still maintains his integrity, though you incited me against him to ruin him without any reason.*

> *4: "Skin for skin!" Satan replied. "A man will give all he has for his own life.*

> *5: But now stretch out your hand and strike his flesh and bones and he will surely curse you to your face."*

> *6: The Lord said to Satan, "Very well, then, he is in your hands; but you must spare his life."*

From this debate we learn that God is proud of Job for maintaining his integrity during hard times. God loves it when his children are able to resist Satan. However Satan does not give up very easily. He tells God that surely Job will curse Him if it meant saving his own life. Once again, God gives Satan the power to test Job again.

Satan inflicted Job's body with painful sores from his head to his feet and Job's wife told him to curse God. *"Are you still maintaining your integrity? Curse God and die!"* (Job 2:9). Job's wife was angry and bitter, which stems from selfishness. She had lost everything with Job and could not understand why he had not already cursed God. Job's response was, *"Shall we accept good from God, and not trouble?"* (Job 2:10).

Do we expect nothing but good things to from God? Jesus tells us in the Word in John 16:33, we will have tribulations. Therefore we should thank God for the good and the bad. Everything God gives us is a gift from him, whether it is good or bad, it is still a gift. Every good gift and every perfect gift is from above, and cometh down from the father of lights, with whom is no variableness, neither shadow of turning (James 1:17). Many times, we only turn to God when things are going bad. He may be causing what we may perceive to be bad things to happen in your life so that you can turn and seek His wisdom and guidance. Everything He does is all a part of His master plan.

"Give thanks in all circumstances; for this is God's will for you in Christ Jesus" 1 Thessalonians 5:18 (New International Version)

Satan used Job's wife in his attack on Job. Satan wanted him to curse God and he used the wife to deliver the message. Satan is not above using the people closest to you to attack you. He will use your spouse, your children, your parents, your siblings, and even your friends. Those are some of the various avenues in which he comes. Satan loves to attack the people of God through marriages and relationships because he knows that we are emotionally attached to certain people, therefore he uses them to hurt us. When we try to place temporary people in permanent positions in our lives, that's where a lot of our heartache enters. Not every relationship or marriage will be perfect but if it is anointed and ordained by God, then together it can conquer anything. Satan uses every trick and strategy in his book to come after God's children. He attacks us in ways that we do not see coming. Satan forms many weapons against us, but we must take comfort in God's word.

> *"No weapon forged against you will prevail, and*
> *you will refute every tongue that accuses you."*
> *Isaiah 54:17 (New International Version)*

Many are misled by that verse. It does not say that Satan will not attack you because he will. He will form many weapons to attack you and he usually uses people to do it. People will be evil and deceitful and not realize they are being used by the enemy. They will try to hurt in you in any way possible, but it is not them that with whom we should become angry. It is the spirit that is manipulating them to do those things. We wrest not against the flesh and blood (Ephesians 6:12). Those attacks may cause you heartache and pain, and you may have lonely days and sleepless nights because of it. People may slander you and drag your reputation through the mud. They may even judge you. But in the end, their attacks or weapons will not destroy you and God shall condemn everyone that judged you. Regardless of what happens, do not sacrifice your integrity by stooping to their level. God will handle your battles if you will just give Him complete control. Vengeance is mine says the Lord. (Romans 12:19)

Despite his circumstances and all that Job had lost and endured, he still refused to curse God, despite his circumstances. Three of his friends, Eliphaz, Bildad, and Zophar, came and sat with Job in silence for seven days and seven nights out of respect for his mourning. On the seventh day, Job begins a conversation with each of them. He still doesn't curse God but he curses the day he was born. *"May the day of my birth perish, and the night that said, "A boy is conceived!" That day-may it turn to darkness."* (Job 3:3-4). Job's friends are convinced that Job's suffering was caused by his own sins against God. Bildad believed that Job's children brought their deaths upon themselves. Job became angry with them. Although they were considered men of God, Job told them that he was not inferior to them and he can argue his own case with God. (Job 13:2-3). Job knew in his heart he had not sin against God. He does not curse God but he does begin to question God as any person in his situation would.

From the moment a child learns to speak and talk, they begin asking "Why?" They want to know *why* the sky is blue. *Why* does a dog bark? *Why* this and *why* that? They will ask over a million "why" questions because, as little children, they are curious. As adults, we often make up answers because we really do not know some of the answers ourselves. Most of the times we just want the child to stop asking us so many questions. The most commonly used parental answer to many *"Why"* questions is simply "Because I said so."

As a child, I would wonder, *Why do I have to make my bed up if I was going to get back in it later?* I actually asked my mother that question one day and her answer was, *Because I said so.* I continued to make my bed up most days because she "said so" even though I never got the answer to my question. When I had my own children, I finally understood why my mother answered me that way. She wanted my obedience and for me not to question her reasoning. It was not for me to understand why. I was just supposed to follow orders because she was my mother and I was her child.

It is the same way with God. We often want to question why things happen or why He let things happen in our lives. It is human nature to question things we do not understand. There are times however, that God doesn't want our questions, He wants our obedience. He wants us to just trust in Him. Trust that He is doing what's in our best interest. We want God to fix certain things in our lives but we want Him to do it our way. That is not how God operates. His way is always the best way.

"As for God, his way is perfect; The Lord's word is flawless; he shields all who take refuge in him." II Samuel 22:31 (New International Version)

As mentioned before, we will all experience some degree of difficulty, tests trials, tribulations or heartache; and we all go through times when we want to know *why* something has happened to us. When my daughter died, I asked God, "Why?" Why did you take her from me? Why did she have to die? Why give her to me if you were only going to take her back in two years? Just simply, "Why God?" God has his own way of revealing the answers in His own timing. With God, nothing happens by chance. Everything has a time, a purpose and a plan. Years later, I finally got the answers to my questions. I believe that my daughter was taken from me because it was the only way that I would have gotten out of the toxic relationship that I was in with her father. I had suffered physical, verbal and emotional abuse while in that relationship. The reason I stayed so long was because of my daughter. We both grew up in households where our parents stayed together through everything, and we wanted that for our daughter. God had given me signs prior to my daughter's passing, that I needed to leave, but I constantly ignored them. This was not the man that God had placed on this earth for me, but I kept trying to place him in a permanent status. If I had stayed in the relationship, one of us would have been dead and the other would be in jail. Taking my child was God's way of altering my life course. It took some years before I received my answers, but I thank God for revealing His purpose to me, and I am at peace with it now. Even though we sometimes question God, we must be patient and wait for His answer to be revealed. The answer may come after some time or it may never come. Either way, God is still in control.

Job had a fourth friend there named Elihu. Elihu became angry with Job and his three friends. Job was too busy justifying himself to his friends rather than justifying God. His three friends had no proof that Job had committed any sin against God but they were convinced that God would never allow anyone to suffer so much pain and agony unless they had offended Him severely in some way. His friends criticized and condemned him. (Job 32:2-3). Many times when people are judging others, they spend much time, effort and energy trying to prove everyone else wrong. Whether they have proof or not, they will judge anyway. Most times, people judge and condemn others because their lives are in a total mess and condemning others makes them feel better about their own messed up situations. They want to take the spotlight off of their issues and shine it brightly on issues of others. We need to keep our focus on God and He will handle those that judge others.

Elihu spoke to Job about the wonders of God. In chapter 38:1, it reads, *Then the Lord spoke to Job out of the storm.* God wanted Job to be brave and answer his questions. God asked questions to show Job how little he knew about creation and how much power God Himself has. He asked Job in verse four: *Where were you when I laid the earth's foundation?* Verse five: *Who marked off its dimensions?* God asked Job a series of questions from Chapters 38 and 39. In chapter 40:3-4- *I am unworthy. How can I reply to you?* God continued to question Job until Chapter 42. Job acknowledges that God's power is infinite well beyond human comprehension. *I know that you can do all things; no purpose of yours can be thwarted.* (42:1). God then becomes angry at Job's three friends for condemning him and giving him unsound, unsubstantiated advice. Job asks God to forgive them and he does.

"After Job prayed for his friends, the LORD restored his fortunes and gave him TWICE as much as he had before." Job 42:10 (New International Version)

It would behoove us as children of God to be more like Job. He was a good and faithful servant. God blessed him with twice as much as he had before. Job suffered mentally, physically and emotionally, and lost so much, but he recognized that God had unlimited power beyond human comprehension. God blessed the end of Job's life more than his beginning. It would be wise for us to not get caught up on the things we have lost. In spite of it all, we must trust that God is in control and that He will bless us with even more than we had before if we just believe that it is in His perfect will for our lives. Just as God was able to bless Job, if you just trust and believe, he can do the same for you.

Blessed are they that mourn, for they shall be comforted.

Lessons Learned

- Do we expect nothing but good things from God?
- Satan is not above using the people closest to you to attack you. He will use your friends, your spouse, your children, your siblings, and even your parents.
- Not every relationship or marriage will be perfect but if it is anointed and ordained by God, then together it can conquer anything.
- God will handle your battles if you will just give Him complete control. Vengeance is mine says the Lord (Romans 12:19).
- We often want to question why things happen or why He let things happen in our lives. It is human nature to question things we do not understand.

TWICE AS MUCH

And I will restore to you the years that the locust hath eaten,
the cankerworm, and the caterpillar, and the palmerworm,
my great army which I sent among you (Joel 2:25).

When I lost my daughter in 2006, I felt that my life was over. I could see no way of going on; but God had bigger and better plans in store for my life. On December 16, 2007, the Lord blessed me with a beautiful son, Keenan Levon Breland-Smith. During my time of struggle and transition, I sought comfort in the arms of close friend and former high school sweetheart. Finding out that I was pregnant with Keenan was the most wonderful feeling in the world for me! I felt as though I had been given a second chance at motherhood. The Lord took my pain and turned it into joy. The hurt from losing my daughter was still there and her memory will forever remain deeply imbedded in my heart, but God gave me my joy back through the birth of a bouncing baby boy! He saved me from a life of self-destruction when he gave me that second child. I was grateful for my new son because I was able to channel my energies towards raising and caring for him. When he was three months old, I met and fell in love with my husband, Myron Smith. We married a few months later on July 8, 2008. God blessed me with a wonderful God-loving husband and father. He is the love of my life and the man that was placed on this earth just for me. He is my help and soul mate and one of my greatest blessings. On September 21, 2009, the Lord blessed us with twins, Myron Ruel Smith, Jr and Kee'undra Louvenia Smith. In the midst of my pain, I was not able to see the Hand of the Lord in my life, not could I see better days, but when God is navigating your life, all things work out for your good. When I became pregnant with our twins, my husband and I decided that this would be our final pregnancy. Unless God has other plans for me, I don't plan on having any more children. My husband wanted a girl and I wanted a boy. God gave us both. God's wonder is truly amazing, and in spite of what I have been through, He never left me. He comforted me, taught me a lesson, then blessed me. I never would have guessed in a million years that I would give birth to twins. Although our twins came two months premature and stayed in the hospital an extra month, they are still healthy and happy children today. It was a week before I was able to hold them in my arms. The doctors kept telling us that twins do not normally go home together. One always stays in the hospital longer than the other, but the doctor did not know that my God had the final say so. We brought both of our babies home from the hospital the same day which was the first time that had ever happened at that particular hospital. I knew that God was in the midst of it all. Needless-to-say, I love my children with my whole heart. They can never take replace of the child that I lost but I take comfort in knowing that it was God's plan. He wanted to direct my life towards a different path. Because I trusted and believed, He gave me back twice as much as I had before, and more. I now know from experience that He is still in the blessing business. I have learned not to take things for granted, but to just simply trust God. He knows what He is doing. When God allows us to lose things, He always has a better replacement. He never takes without replacing. Whenever you lose, you are still gaining. Stop trying to hold on to the very thing that God is trying to take.

Trying to control God is something that will stifle your spiritual journey. Many times when we pray to God, we come with instructions on how we want Him to fix our situation. When we pray, God doesn't want nor does He need your instructions. He just wants us to simply relinquish our hearts to Him. While we are busy trying to figure it all out, God has already worked it out. We spend energy and time stressing over things that God has already taken care of. Our time and energy can be devoted to our families, our ministry or doing other productive things. Everyone has a story and a testimony. All may not share theirs, but everyone has some experience that they have overcome. Don't be afraid to share your journey with others. You will find that in your story, is a blessing that may set someone free! God does not always call the qualified, but He does qualify those that He calls.

GOD IS TRYING TO TELL YOU SOMETHING

When I was younger, I saw a movie called, 'The Color Purple' starring Whoopi Goldberg. My favorite part of the movie was the end when Shug Avery started singing a song entitled, 'God is trying to tell you something.' For years I never understood the deeper meaning of the song. Sometimes God is trying to tell us something but we get so busy with life and living that we never stop and listen. A verse in the song says, *You can't sleep at night, and you wonder why, Maybe God is trying to tell you something.* God wants us to take the time and be still.

> *Be still, and know that I am God. Psalms*
> *46:10 (New International Version)*

Life is busy for most people. Sometimes it can be overwhelming, but we must take the time to just be still and listen to God. Most of the time when we come to God, we come telling Him our problems. God already knows what our problems are. He created us. He knows our situations. He knows the storms that we are facing. He knows our trials and tribulations. He knows everything about us. In Jeremiah 1:5, it states, *Before I formed you in the womb I knew you.* This means that before you were even conceived, God knew you. He knows our heart's desires, thoughts, behaviors and circumstances. Therefore, we don't need to come to God with our problems, we come to Him with our worship and praise. As with Job, God has the power to speak to us out of the storm. When you trust God with your whole heart, a sense of peace and calmness will take over your heart and mind. It is not necessary to tell God how big your problems are because He already knows. What you should do is tell your problems how big your God is. God can do things that we cannot in our natural mind imagine or understand. God can open a door that we never knew was there. There is no limit to God's power, which is why He is infinite and unlimited and we are finite and limited. God wants us to take the time to be still. He just wants a few minutes of our time each day. Before I started trusting God, I couldn't sleep at night. I had insomnia so badly that I was taking a sleep medication called Ambien just so I could sleep every night. Life was stressful and hard to bear at that time. I would stay up all night trying to figure out how to fix my situation, but when I started trusting God, I started sleeping peacefully at night. Once I put everything into God's hands, I didn't need any more sleeping pills in order to get rest. God had to place me in a situation where I could be still in order to hear from Him, see clearly, and get peace. Once I was still, I was able to hear what He was trying to tell me. I no longer come to God with my problems. I come thanking and worshipping Him for all that he has done, for all that He is doing and for all that He is going to do in my life. The bible is filled with instances of God giving twice as much as before. Take an inventory of your own life. Just sit back and think of what your life was like before you totally gave your life to Christ and how far He has brought you. His grace and mercy will protect you always. Just be still and listen to what God is trying to tell you.

When you feel like complaining, just think of how different things could be. There is someone out there who wishes they had what you have. Before you complain about hating your job, remember that there is someone who wishes they had a job. Before you complain about not getting any relaxation time because of the children keeping you up at night, remember there are thousands of couples who would do anything to have a child. Life can be hard and unpredictable. People may have written you off and told you that you would never amount to anything. Sometimes we have more bills than money. Doctors may have given up hope. Everyone's situation and circumstances are different, but in spite of what you are going through, Trust God. Words can hurt and even sink down into the belief system, but trust God and seek His validation. Whatever the situation, please know that it is all a part of God's holy plan. We must have tunnel vision and keep our focus on God. We must run our own race and not get so consumed with things of this world. Pray for others as well as yourself. Live your life in a way that God would be honored and pleased. We all make mistakes. That is a part of being human. We all have sinned and fallen down. However, as long as we get back up and keep trying, the devil will not win.

I pray that this book has given you some encouragement during your situation. Just remember that God loves you. He made you in His image. God makes no mistakes. The pain that you have been feeling cannot compare to the joy that is coming.

For I consider that the sufferings of this present time are not worthy to be compared with the glory which shall be revealed in us. Romans 8:18 (New King James Version)

Lessons Learned

- God is still in the blessing business.
- God never takes without replacing. Whenever you lose, you are still gaining.
- Be still and wait on the Lord.

About the Author

 Keeba Smith was born and raised in Laurel, MS. She is the third and youngest child to Kenneth and Nancy Breland. Keeba graduated from Laurel High School in 1998 and joined the U. S. Army in 1999. She served in the military for a total of eight years both in active and national guard duty. She has an Associate's Degree in Business Education from Jones County Junior College, a Bachelor's Degree in Psychology from Middle Tennessee State University and a Master's Degree in Elementary Education from Jackson State University.

Keeba currently resides in Ellisville, MS with her husband, Myron. Together they have 3 children; Keenan, Myron Jr. and Kee'undra. She currently works as a freelance writer. She also loves history and traveling. She is looking for a way to bless others during their struggles.

Contact Information:

Phone: 601-498-5299
Email: keebasmith@yahoo.com
Twitter: @motherof3smiths